C.S.I.
BANK ROBBERY

John Townsend

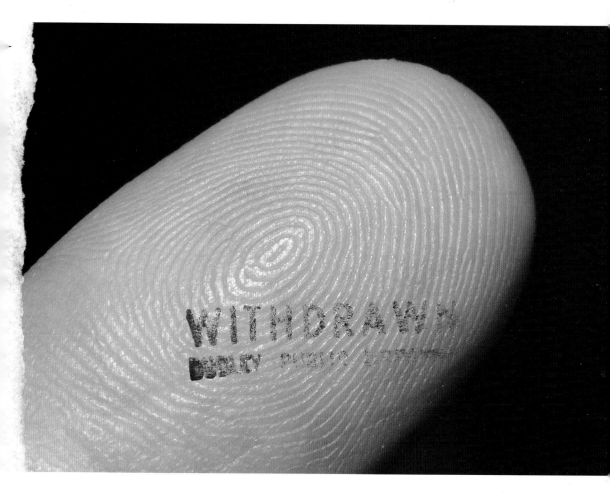

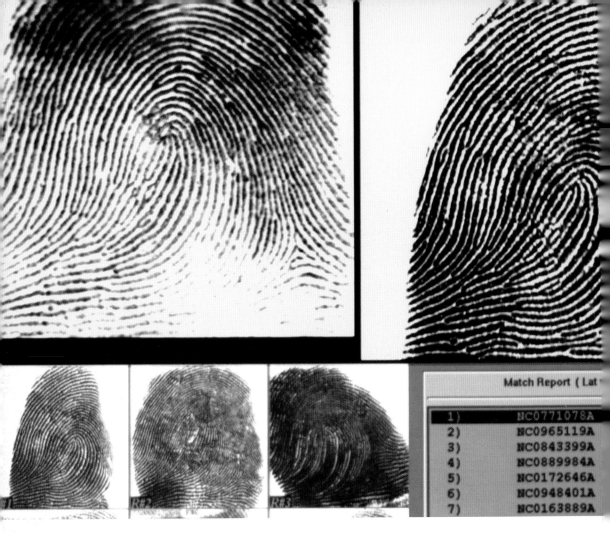

Copyright © ticktock Entertainment Ltd 2008

First published in Great Britain in 2008 by ticktock Media Ltd,
2 Orchard Business Centre, North Farm Road, Tunbridge Wells, Kent, TN2 3XF

ticktock project editor: Ruth Owen
ticktock project designer: Sara Greasley
ticktock picture researcher: Lizzie Knowles

**With thanks to series editors Honor Head and Jean Coppendale,
and consultant John Cassella, Principal Lecturer in Forensic Science, Staffordshire University, UK**

Thank you to Lorraine Petersen and the members of nasen

ISBN 978 1 84696 713 9 pbk

Printed in China

A CIP catalogue record for this book is available from the British Library.

Picture credits (t=top; b=bottom; c=centre; l=left; r=right):
Michael Donne/ Science Photo Library: 7, 22b. Martin Dohrn/ Science Photo Library: 8-9. Mauro Fermariello/ Science
Photo Library: 12, 13. David R. Frazier/ Science Photo Library: 25t. Mitsuaki Iwago/ Minden Pictures/ FLPA: 11br.
James King-Holmes/ Science Photo Library: 15 main, 16, 18-19 main. Pasieka/ Science Photo Library: OFC. Philippe
Psaila/ Science Photo Library: 17b, 21t, 21b. Paul Rapson/ Science Photo Library: 6. Shutterstock: 1, 2, 4-5 all, 10 all,
11t, 11cr, 11bl, 14, 15t, 17t, 19t, 20 all, 22t, 23t, 23b, 25b, 27, 28 all, 29 all, 31 all. Upper Cut Images/ Getty Images:
24. Jim Varney/ Science Photo Library: 26.

Every effort has been made to trace copyright holders, and we apologise in advance for any omissions. We would be
pleased to insert the appropriate acknowledgments in any subsequent edition of this publication.

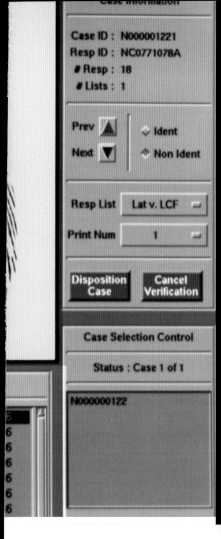

Case ID : N000001221
Resp ID : NC0771078A
Resp : 18
Lists : 1

Prev ▲   ◇ Ident
Next ▼   ◆ Non Ident

Resp List   Lat v. LCF   ▱

Print Num   1   ▱

Disposition   Cancel
Case   Verification

Case Selection Control

Status : Case 1 of 1

N000000122

Contents

CHAPTER 1

ROBBERY!

"Everybody down on the floor. Now!"

A robber wearing a mask bursts into a bank.

He is carrying a gun. He points the gun to make everyone lie on the floor. He forces the bank workers to put the money into bags.

The police speed to the bank.

The robber gets away with thousands of pounds!

He speeds away from the bank in a getaway car. The car is driven by a second robber. He is also wearing a mask.

The police find the getaway car just outside the city. It has been set on fire. The police think the robbers set fire to the car...

...to destroy all the evidence!

CHAPTER 2

FINGERPRINTS

The car the robbers used was stolen!
The stolen car is now a crime scene.

Crime scene investigators (CSIs) get to work on the car.
They are looking for forensic evidence such as fingerprints.

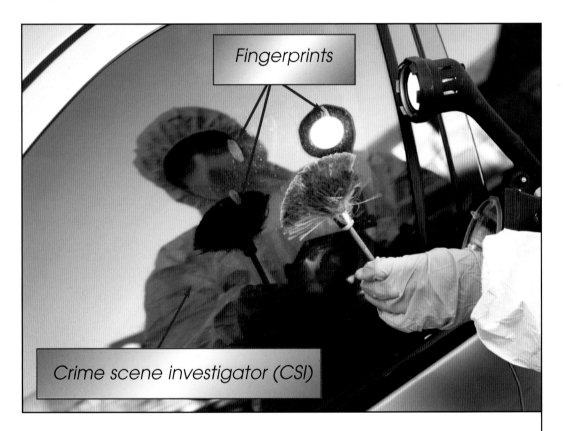

Fingerprints

Crime scene investigator (CSI)

One CSI brushes fingerprint powder onto one of the car's
windows. A special lamp makes the fingerprints show up.

Did the robbers touch the car with their bare hands?
If they did, their sweaty fingers will have left fingerprints.

Another CSI uses sticky tape to lift a fingerprint from one of the car's seatbelts.

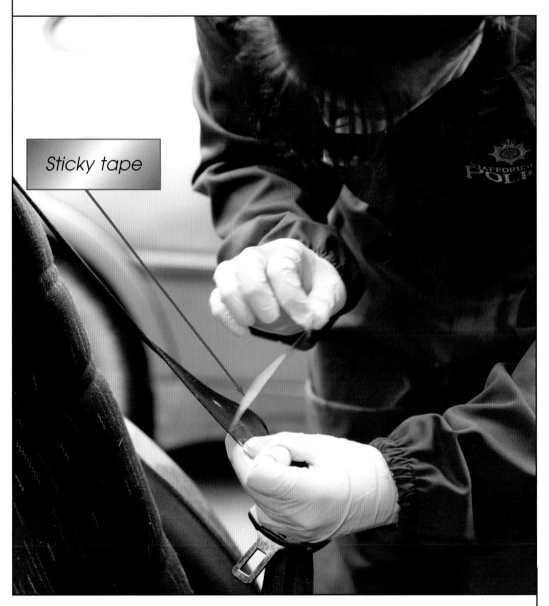

Sticky tape

The tape will be stuck to a piece of card called a lift card.

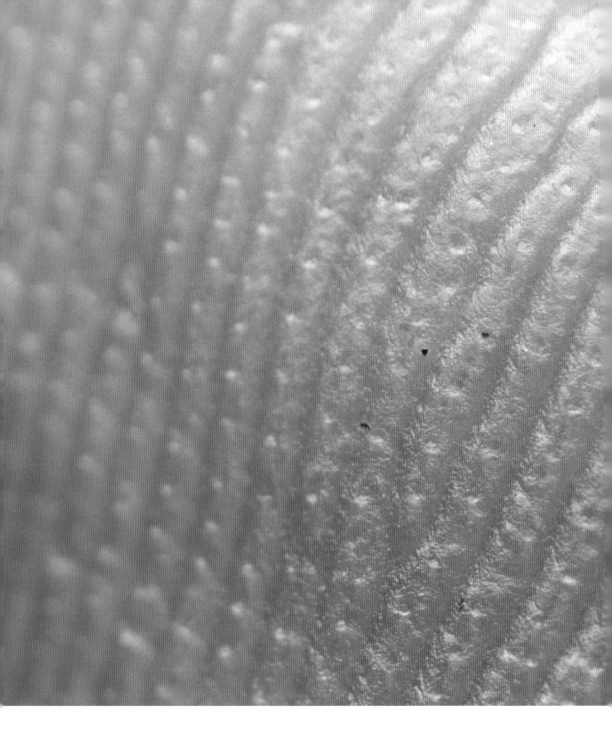

Our fingerprint patterns are made by skin ridges.
The sweat comes from sweat glands.
No two people have the same fingerprint pattern.
Even identical twins have different fingerprints.

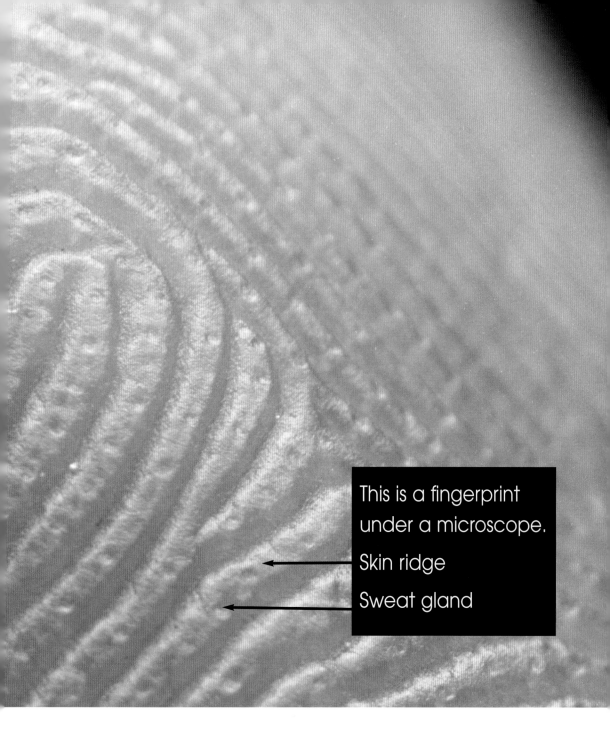

This is a fingerprint under a microscope.

Skin ridge

Sweat gland

Our fingerprints form before we are born.
They stay the same our entire life.
They only change if our fingers are burnt or scarred.

There are three main fingerprint patterns.

Arches

This pattern has ridges which enter from one side of the print and go off the other side. The ridges make an arch shape.

Loops

This pattern has a ridge that starts on one side. It makes a loop then goes back off on the same side.

Whorls

This pattern has ridges that make a complete circle.

Fingerprints have a main pattern and lots of other tiny details.

Dot

Bifurcation

Short ridge

Bridge

Ridge ending

IS THAT A FACT?

Koala fingerprints are just like human prints. Even with a microscope, it's difficult to tell them apart!

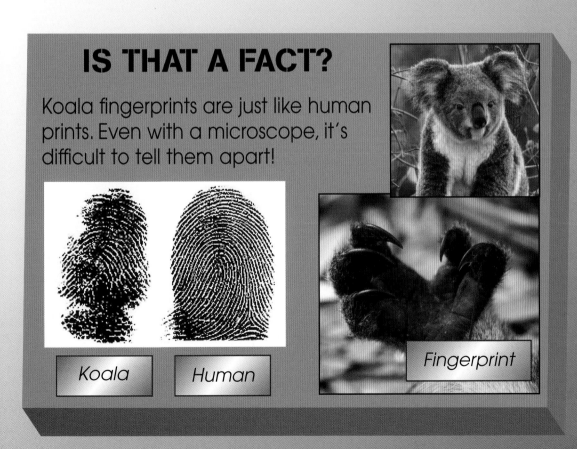

Koala

Human

Fingerprint

CHAPTER 3

AT THE CRIME LAB

The fingerprints found on the car are taken to the crime lab.

First, the fingerprints will be compared with fingerprints from the car owner and his family.

The fingerprints are scanned and put into a computer programme.

Fingerprint expert

A fingerprint expert compares the fingerprint from the seatbelt with one from the car owner. It's a skilful job.

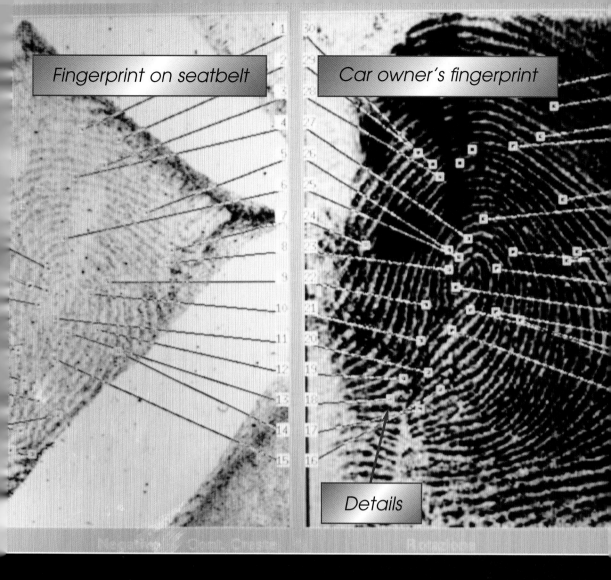

Fingerprint on seatbelt

Car owner's fingerprint

Details

Carefully and closely details on the two prints are compared. They are a match!

RESULT

The fingerprint on the seatbelt wasn't from the robbers. It belongs to the car owner. All the fingerprints on the car are from the owner or his family.

The police find a leather glove near the getaway car.

Could this be a breakthrough?

They check the CCTV film taken at the bank.
The glove is just like one worn by the robber.
The robber thought he was clever wearing gloves.
But guess what the police find on the glove…

…fingerprints!

The prints can be compared to fingerprints
on a police database. This database holds the
fingerprints of thousands of known criminals.

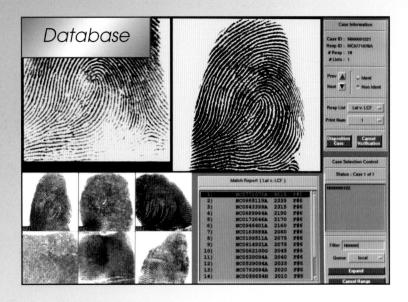

Database

If the bank robbers have committed a crime in the
past, their fingerprints will be on the database.

CCTV film

Leather glove

Fingerprints

RESULT
It's bad news!
The fingerprints on the glove
do not match any on the
police database.

Another way to test for prints is using magnetic powder.

This works on difficult surfaces such as plastic bags, magazines and even fruit.

Tiny iron flakes stick to the print. Then the soft, magnetic brush picks up all the loose flakes. The print made of iron flakes is left behind.

Magnetic brush

Unlike old-fashioned dusting brushes, this brush doesn't touch or harm the print.

Print of iron flakes

The CSIs find a CD in the car. The CD does not belong to the car's owner.

There are fingerprints on the CD.

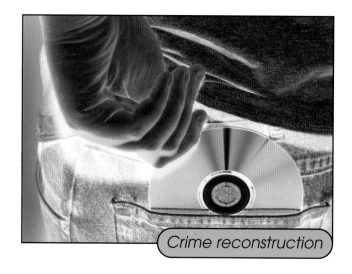

Crime reconstruction

The fingerprints on the CD don't belong to the car owner or his family. They don't match any on the police database. They don't match the prints on the glove. But they do match prints on the car's false number plate.

RESULT
The police think they may have the prints of the second robber who drove the getaway car.

The crime scene investigators keep searching.

Near to the car they find a banana under a hedge.
It's a funny place to find a banana!

Using magnetic powder, they dust the banana skin.
Three fingerprints show up!

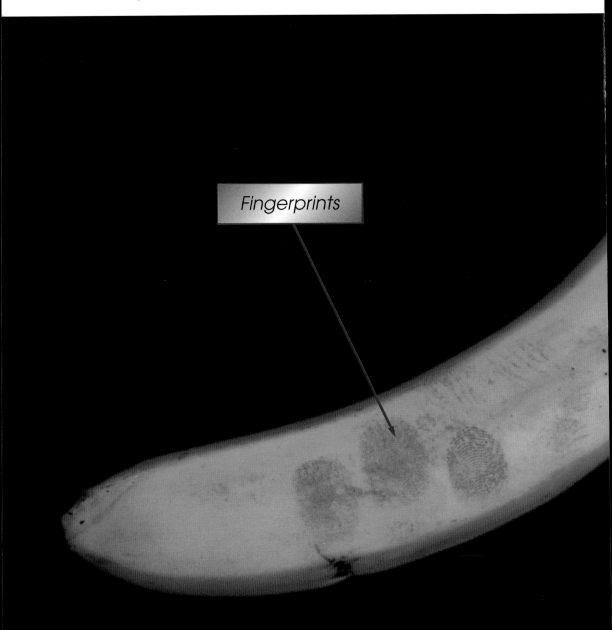

Fingerprints

Did one of the robbers decide he didn't have time for a snack?

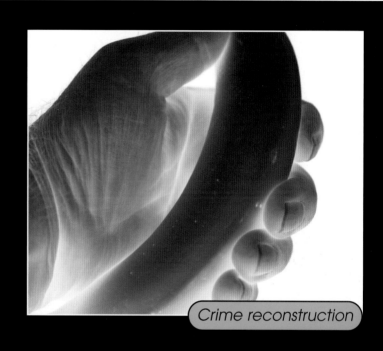

Crime reconstruction

RESULT
The prints on the banana
match the prints on
the glove!

Close to where the CSIs find the banana, they find torn envelopes.

Some of the stolen money was in envelopes.
Fingerprints don't show up on paper.
But a chemical called DFO reacts with sweat from fingers.

At the lab, the torn envelopes are dipped in DFO. Then an ultra-violet light is shone on the paper.

The DFO and ultra-violet light makes fingerprints on paper glow orange.

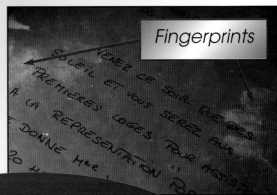

Fingerprints

RESULT
Both robbers' prints are on the torn envelopes. The robbers couldn't wait to count their money!

Crime reconstruction – the robbers tore open the envelopes to count the money!

21

The CSIs make another discovery outside the bank.

Just where the getaway car had been waiting, the CSIs find an empty drinks can.

It has the driver's fingerprints all over it!

Crime reconstruction

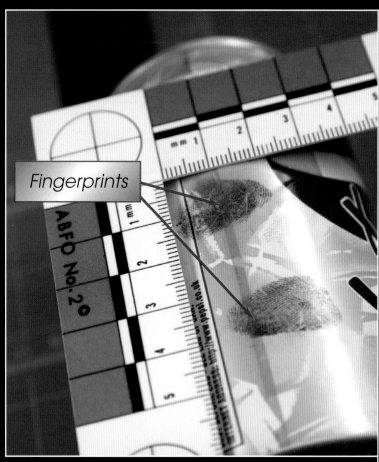

Fingerprints

The can is photographed with measurements.
The photos record the position and size of the prints.

It's not just the driver's fingerprints on the can.
His lip prints are there, too.

Just like our fingerprints, our lip prints are unique, too.

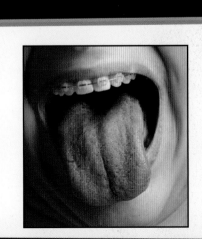

IS THAT A FACT?

Police have caught criminals from prints of their toes, knees, ears and tongues!

CHAPTER 4

AN ARREST!

**The police have prints from the two robbers.
But they have no idea who the men are.**

Then there is a breakthrough!

The police stop a man for driving too fast.
He tries to run off. The police catch and arrest him.

An officer takes his prints with a fingerprinting machine.
It sends the prints straight to the police database.

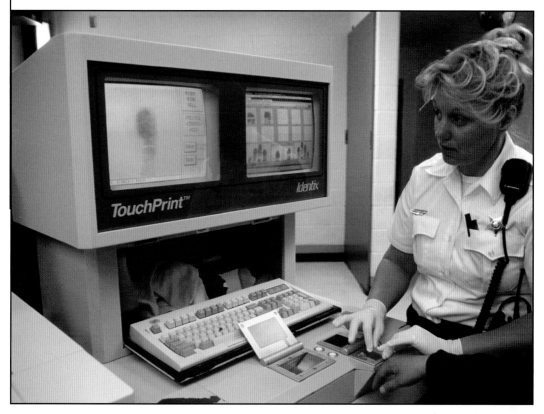

The computer comes back with a message.
The man's prints match one of the bank robber's!

The man's mobile phone leads the police to his friend.
His friend's prints match the other robber's prints.

RESULT
The police
now have
two suspects!

CHAPTER 5

SHOEPRINTS

Both men say they are not the bank robbers. The first man arrested shouts,

"You can't prove I was near that bank."

But the police can!

Sticky gel

The robber left a muddy shoeprint on the floor of the bank. One of the CSIs collected the shoeprint as evidence. He used special paper covered in sticky gel to lift the print.

Just like our
fingerprints,
our shoeprints
are unique, too.

As we walk around,
our shoes get
damaged by stones
or bits of glass.

This damage is unique to our shoes.

RESULT
The shoeprint is matched to
the suspect's shoe. It proves the
suspect was in the bank.

CHAPTER 6

ON TRIAL

In court, the two men are found guilty of the robbery.

Evidence: Suspect A – The Robber	MATCH
Fingerprints on glove by getaway car	✓
Fingerprints on banana by getaway car	✓
Fingerprints on envelopes by getaway car	✓
Shoeprint in the bank	✓

Verdict – prints prove guilt

(Money from the bank robbery is found buried in his garden.)

Evidence: Suspect B – Getaway driver	MATCH
Fingerprints on CD in getaway car	✓
Fingerprints on false number plate of getaway car	✓
Fingerprints on envelopes by getaway car	✓
Fingerprints and lip prints on drinks can outside bank	✓

Verdict – prints prove guilt

CASE SOLVED!

NEED TO KNOW WORDS

bifurcation A fingerprint ridge that is divided into two parts like a Y shape.

crime lab A laboratory with equipment that is used for scientific tests and experiments on crime scene evidence.

crime scene Any place where a crime has happened.

crime scene investigator (CSI) A person who examines crime scenes and collects evidence.

evidence Facts and signs that can show what happened during a crime.

false number plate A made-up registration number on a car. The police cannot trace it.

fingerprint expert An expert at matching fingerprints. They are also known as fingerprint analysts.

fingerprint powder A fine dust that sticks to fingerprints. It makes them show up more clearly.

forensic evidence Detailed facts and signs that can show what happened in a crime.

known criminal A person who has been convicted of a crime in the past. The person's details, such as fingerprints, are kept on a police database.

magnetic Something that attracts iron or steel.

suspect A person who the police think has committed a crime.

sweat gland A part of the skin that gives off sweat through a tiny hole called a pore.

ultra-violet light A special light which shines deep purple. It makes some objects glow in the dark.

unique The only one of its kind.

verdict The final decision of what happened.

NEED TO KNOW PRINT FACTS

- **Visible fingerprints**
  Sometimes fingerprints are patent – you can see them. They can be made in blood or left in a soft surface, such as a piece of chewing gum.

- **Unseen fingerprints**
  Fingerprints that cannot be seen are called latent prints. CSIs use dusting powder or chemicals to turn the print a colour that can be seen.

- **Shoe databases**
  Shoe factories store sole patterns on databases. Investigators can use these databases to match a shoeprint with a sole pattern. This will tell them the make of a shoe.

- **Tyre marks**
  Car tyres make prints in mud and sand. The pattern of the tread can prove what make of tyre made the print. Cuts, holes and worn parts of the tyre will show up, too. This will make each tyre print unique.

PRINTS ONLINE

Websites

http://www.cyberbee.com/whodunnit/fp.html
All you need to know about fingerprints

http://www.fbi.gov/kids/6th12th/6th12th.htm
How the FBI investigates crimes

http://www.howstuffworks.com/csi5.htm
All about the world of CSI

http://www.crimelibrary.com/criminal_mind/forensics/crimescene/6.html
All about crime scene analysis

INDEX